SING through the SEASONS

SING

the plough publishing house

Rifton, New York   1972

through the SEASONS

NINETY-NINE SONGS FOR CHILDREN

Compiled and Edited by the SOCIETY OF BROTHERS

Music Arranged by MARLYS SWINGER

Illustrations by MONELI, SUSANNA, and BIENE

Designed by GILLIAN BARTH

First printing   1972
Second printing 1975

ISBN 87486-006-7
Library of Congress Catalog Card Number 70-164916
Printed at the Plough Press, Farmington, Pa., U.S.A.

Acknowledgements

The Society of Brothers is grateful for the use of copyrighted material granted by the following publishers and authors:

ABINGDON PRESS for permission to reprint and set to music the following three poems from *Winds A'Blowing* by May Justus: "Spring Secret," copyright 1952 by Pierce and Smith (Abingdon Press); "Signs of Spring," copyright © 1961 by Abingdon Press; and "Remember September," copyright © 1947 by May Justus, 1961 by Abingdon Press.

ADDISON-WESLEY PUBLISHING COMPANY for "Nibble Nibble Nibble" from the book *Nibble Nibble* by Margaret Wise Brown, copyright 1959, published by William R. Scott, Inc. Permission to reprint and set to music given by Addison-Wesley Publishing Company, Inc.

ASSOCIATION FOR CHILDHOOD EDUCATION INTERNATIONAL for "Wise Johnny" by Edwina Fallis. From *Sung under the Silver Umbrella*, copyright 1935 by the Macmillan Company, New York, New York. Used by permission.

JOHN BECKER for permission to reprint and set to music "Feather or Fur" from *New Feathers for the Old Goose* by John Becker. New York: Pantheon Books, Inc., 1956.

BELWIN-MILLS PUBLISHING CORP., U.S. agents for Schott and Co., Ltd., for "Under Bethlehem's Star so Bright" ("Shepherds Watched Their Flocks by Night") from *Seven Czechoslovak Carols*, arranged by Vilém Tausky. Copyright 1942 by Schott & Co., Ltd. Copyright renewed 1970 by Schott & Co., Ltd. Used by permission.

THE BODLEY HEAD for "I Pick up My Hoe," traditional, edited by Elizabeth Poston, published in *The Children's Song Book*.

COOPERATIVE RECREATION SERVICE, INC., for "Out in the Meadows" from *Joyful Singing*; "The Winter Now Is Over" from *Songs to Keep*; "Susani" from *Little Book of Carols*; "Potato Harvest" from *Sing a Tune*, copyright 1966; "Paddling My Canoe" from *Songs of the Wigwam*, copyright 1955; and "Swinging Along" from *Chansons de Notre Chalet*, copyright 1957, 1959, 1962.

IVY O. EASTWICK and THE PLOUGH PUBLISHING HOUSE for "A Happy Goodmorning," "I Can't See the Wind," "On Silver Sands," and "Winter-Walk" from *In and Out the Windows*, copyright 1969 by Ivy O. Eastwick and The Plough Publishing House.

EVANS BROTHERS, LTD., for "Daffodillies" by A.W.I. Chitty from *Movement and Song for the Junior School* and *Child Education*, and for the music only of "Jack Frost" by Ivor Davies.

FOLLETT PUBLISHING COMPANY for "Come Out! Come Out!" and "Autumn Roundelay" from *Music Sounds Afar* from the Together We Sing Series. Copyright 1958 by Follett Publishing Company. Used by permission of Follett Publishing Company.

W. J. GAGE LTD. for "Lippity-Lop" and "Jack-o'-Lantern" from *The New High Road of Song for Nursery Schools and Kindergartens*, copyright 1960 by The Canada Publishing Co., Ltd., Toronto.

GALAXY MUSIC CORP. for "Willow's Lullaby" from *Sing-Song from Sweden*, published by Augener, Ltd., succeeded by Galliard, Ltd., London, represented in U.S. by Galaxy Music Corp.

TOM GLAZER for "Today Is Your Birthday," words and music by Tom Glazer, copyright 1952, assigned to Songs Music, Inc., Scarborough, New York.

GROSSET & DUNLAP, INC., for "Rhyme" from *The Sparrow Bush* by Elizabeth Coatsworth. Text copyright © by W. W. Norton & Company, Inc. Published by Grosset & Dunlap, Inc.

LOIS LENSKI for permission to use "I Like Winter" from *I Like Winter* by Lois Lenski, published by Henry Z. Walck, Inc., copyright 1950.

WILLIAM MORRIS AGENCY for the English Commonwealth rights for reprinting "Three Little Puffins" from *The Silver Curlew* by Eleanor Farjeon, copyright 1953 by Eleanor Farjeon, published by Viking Press, Inc. Reprinted by permission of William Morris Agency, Inc.

OXFORD UNIVERSITY PRESS for "Rocking," "The Birds" and "Easter Eggs" from *The Oxford Book of Carols*. Also for permission to reprint and set to music "Willows in the Snow" and "Crocuses" from *A Year of Japanese Epigrams*, translated by William N. Porter and published by Oxford University Press.

Acknowledgements

G. Schirmer, Inc., for "Hiawatha" from *Hiawatha Dramatized* by H.A. Donald, published by Curwen and Sons, Ltd. Used by permission of G. Schirmer, Inc., representatives in the U.S.A. of Curwen.

Schmitt, Hall & McCreary Company for "January and February" from *The Golden Book of Favorite Songs*. Used by permission of the publishers. Also for verses 2 and 3 of "All the Birds" ("The Birds' Return") from *The Golden Book of Favorite Songs*.

Charles Scribner's Sons for "Time for Rabbits" and "Caterpillars" from *Cricket in a Thicket* by Aileen Fisher. Copyright © 1963 by Aileen Fisher. Permission to reprint and set to music given by Charles Scribner's Sons.

Nancy Byrd Turner for permission to reprint and set to music "Winter Sports" and "Popcorn Song."

The Viking Press for permission to reprint and set to music "Three Little Puffins" from *The Silver Curlew* by Eleanor Farjeon, copyright 1953 by Eleanor Farjeon. Reprinted by permission of The Viking Press, Inc.

Frederick Warne and Company for "Little Wind" from *Under the Window* by Kate Greenaway. Reprinted and set to music by permission of Frederick Warne and Company.

A. P. Watt & Son for "The Little Tune" by Rose Fyleman. Reprinted and set to music by permission of The Estate of Rose Fyleman.

The Willis Music Company for verse 1 of "All the Birds Sing up in the Trees" ("All the Birds Are Singing Again") from *Songs for the Nursery School* by Laura Pendleton MacCarteney.

Wonderland Music Company, Inc., for "Little April Shower," words by Larry Morey, music by Frank Churchill. Copyright 1942 by Wonderland Music Company, Inc. Used by permission.

Every effort has been made to find all sources of the material in this book. Any necessary corrections will be made in future editions.

Introduction

A child's keen eye sees and his ear is attuned to each new sound; he cannot keep his feet still, his hands off, or his voice silent! And children will sing! Even when tucked in bed, with the lights turned off and a last goodnight said, how often will a child sing himself to sleep!

In the life with our children in the communities of the Society of Brothers, each day has its accompaniment of song. Out of this we compiled our first songbook, *Sing Through the Day*.

That was only a small part of our store, however. We look forward as well to each season as it comes, partly at least, for the songs that go with it, old ones we enjoy singing again, new ones we find or make up ourselves. In all four of our communities we live in the country, close to nature and to the cycle of the year.

This present book, *Sing Through the Seasons*, is a collection of the seasonal songs that we especially enjoy. Some are from poems by well-known and well-loved authors—Eleanor Farjeon, Elizabeth Coatsworth, Aileen Fisher, Ivy Eastwick. Others were written in the community, like "Where Are the Froggies?"—incidentally a lesson in hibernation—composed by our kindergarten group. Some folk songs appear here for the first time in English translation, like "O Snowflake, White Snowflake" and "O Fir Tree Tall." Some songs may be well-known, such as

Introduction

"Willie, Bring Your Little Drum." The illustrations are done by three of our young members as in *Sing Through the Day*.

If you discover this book as a teacher, we wish you many hours of pleasure with it as you live around the calendar with your children. If the book reaches your hands as a parent, our hope is that it will enrich your life as a family.

Jane Tyson Clement

For those unfamiliar with our books, the Plough Publishing House is part of the Society of Brothers, or Bruderhof, a group of families and single people living in Christian community since 1920, when our life together began in Sannerz, Germany. One of our books, *Torches Together*, by Emmy Arnold, tells the story of our earlier years. Driven from Germany by Nazi persecution, the community continued in England; because of our large number of German members we had to leave England in 1941 (except for a tiny group), taking refuge in Paraguay. In 1954 we made our first beginning in North America, where at the moment we have three communities: Woodcrest at Rifton, New York; New Meadow Run at Farmington, Pennsylvania; and Deer Spring at Norfolk, Connecticut. In 1971 we settled again in England at our Darvell Community near Robertsbridge, Sussex. We support ourselves with the manufacture and sale of children's toys, Community Playthings. We welcome inquiries and visits. Please contact us in advance.

We rejoice with children in their delight in nature. The child senses the light of God behind the stars that flame in the sky. He senses the living creative Spirit when he sees the flowers swaying in the breeze. In the mutual love of human beings and in the love that is in his own child heart, he senses the mystery of God's love, the Source of all life. To the genuine child, love is nothing other than creative and selfless surrender to joy.

Eberhard Arnold

Contents

SING A SONG OF SPRING

Songs originating with the Plough Publishing House are designated *Original*.

ON A SUMMER MORNING

REMEMBER SEPTEMBER

I LIKE WINTER

ALL THAT HATH LIFE AND BREATH

Sing a Song of Spring

Sing a Song of Spring

Edith Möller
English lyrics by Antonia Ridge

F. W. Möller

When the green buds show, And the March winds blow, And the
Warm will shine the sun, Far from home we'll run, Greet-ing

birds all call A-cross the mead-ow, Gay as bird on wing, We'll go
ev-'ry-one So kind and friend-ly. As we go we'll sing, Tell the

wan-der-ing Sing a song of Spring The wide world o-ver. Tra la
world it's Spring, Make sweet ech-oes ring The wide world o-ver. Tra la

la la la la la, Tra la la la la la la, Tra la la la la la la, The wide world o-ver.
la la la la la, Tra la la la la la la, Tra la la la la la la, The wide world o-ver.

New Songs Ring with Gladness

3 Part Round

Translated

German Folk Song

Brightly

New songs ring with glad-ness, For Spring ends all sad-ness; Once more hear the mer-ry bag-pipes Of shep-herds up-on the hill. Tra la la la la la la la la, La la la la la la la la.

All the Birds Sing

Vs. 1 – Laura Pendleton MacCarteney
Vs. 2 and 3 – Jane B. Walters

German Folk Song

Merrily

1. All the birds sing up in the trees: Now the Spring is com - ing!
2. All the birds are here a - gain With their hap-py voic - es;
3. On the ground and in the air, See their colors flash - ing;

Lis-ten, lis-ten, what do they say? Spring-time is the time to be gay!
Nois-y spar-row, wren so bright, Chirp and sing from morn till night,
Rob-in dear, with breast of red, Scratch-ing in the gar - den bed,

All the birds sing up in the trees: Now the Spring is com - ing!
Tell - ing us of Spring's de - light; Ev - 'ry-one re - joic - es.
Blue - bird call - ing o - ver - head, To and fro they're dash - ing.

4

Little April Shower

Larry Morey

Frank Churchill

Lightly

Drip, drip, drop, lit-tle A-pril show-er, Beat-ing a tune ev-'ry-where that you fall.

Drip, drip, drop, lit-tle A-pril show-er, We're get-ting wet and we don't care at all.

Drip! Drop! Drip! Drop! We're get-ting wet and we don't care at all.

It's Raining
("Raining in Holland")

Translated from the Dutch by
Marion Bergman

Dutch Folk Song

It's rain-ing, it's rain-ing, The roofs are get-ting wet. The

rain will make the flow-ers bloom, The mud we'll sweep out with a broom. It's

rain-ing, it's rain-ing, The roofs are get-ting wet.

Where Are the Froggies?

Words and Music
New Meadow Run Children

Briskly

mf

1. Where are the frog-gies when the north winds blow? We can-not see them in the
2. Where are the tur-tles when the north winds blow? We can-not see them in the
3. Where are the bears when the north winds blow? We can-not see them in the

p

ice and snow. Deep, deep down in the mud they lie, Frog-gies sleep-ing with
ice and snow. Deep, deep down in the mud they lie, Tur-tles sleep-ing with
ice and snow. Snug and warm in a cave they lie, Ba-by bears sleep-ing with

f

tight-closed eyes. When the warm spring sun comes out, Frog-gies wake and
tight-closed eyes. When the warm spring sun comes out, Tur-tles wake and
tight-closed eyes. When the warm spring sun comes out, Baby bears wake and

jump a-bout. Oh, how hap-py they will be — A spring-time world they will see!
crawl a-bout. Oh, how hap-py they will be — A spring-time world they will see!
run a-bout. Oh, how hap-py they will be — A spring-time world they will see!

8

*Encourage your children to make up their own verses —
then watch how they enjoy themselves.*

4. Where are the squirrels when the north winds blow?
We cannot see them in the ice and snow.
   Cracking nuts in a hollow tree,
   Squirrels are cozy as cozy can be.
   When the warm spring sun comes out,
   Squirrels wake and jump about.
   Oh, how happy they will be —
   A springtime world they will see!

5. Where are the caterpillars when the north winds blow?
We cannot see them in the ice and snow.
   Snug and warm in a cocoon they lie,
   Caterpillars changing to a butterfly.
   When the warm spring sun comes out,
   Butterflies wake and flutter about.
   Oh, how happy they will be —
   A springtime world they will see!

I Can't See the Wind

Ivy O. Eastwick

Marlys Swinger

Swayingly

I can't see the Wind, but the Wind can see me—it fol-lows me, danc-ing, a-

cross Lan-tern-lea, it blows round my ank-les, it puffs through my hair, it

tan-gles me up till I do not know where or whith-er or thith-er or

why I'm this way, the way of the Wind on a mer-ry March day.

10

Blow Wind, Blow, and Go Mill, Go

Mother Goose

Slovak Folk Tune

Blow wind, blow, and go mill, go, That the mil-ler may grind his

corn;___ That the bak-er may take it, And in - to bread bake it, And

bring us a loaf in the morn,___ And bring us a loaf in the morn.

The Sugar Camp

English paraphrase
Frances Densmore

Based on
Chippewa Melody

Like a chant

1. Let us go____ to the sug-ar camp While the snow lies
2. Cut a notch__ in the ma-ple tree, Set a pail on the
3. Make a fire__ in the sug-ar lodge So that we may
4. In the snow__ see the rab-bit tracks, Hear the note of the

on the ground, Live____ in the birch-bark wig - wam,
ground be-low. Soon the sap____ will be flow - ing,
boil the sap. Bring____ all the wood-en la - dles,
chick-a-dee. We____ must not stop to fol-low them,

All the chil-dren and the old-er folk, While the peo-ple are at work.
From the tree it will be flow - ing. All the peo-ple are at work.
Set the wood-en trough for grain - ing. All the peo-ple are at work.
'Tis the seas-on of the sug-ar camp. All the peo-ple are at work.

5. Bring the sap from the maple trees,
   Pour the sap in the iron pot.
   See how it steams and bubbles.
   May we have a little taste of it?
   All the people are at work.

6. Pour the syrup in the graining trough,
   Stir it slowly as it thicker grows.
   Now it has changed to sugar.
   We may eat it in a birchbark dish.
   There is sugar for us all.

Signs of Spring

May Justus   Marlys Swinger

Cheerfully

I know, I know, I know it— The Spring is here at last.— There's dogwood on the

hill — side, And red-bud com — ing fast.— Wake rob-in's in the deep woods, And

wild ger-a - ni- um.—— I know, I know, I know it— The love-ly Spring has come!—

Spring Secret

May Justus

Vonnie Burleson

Secretly

No - bod-y knows what I know— No - bod-y knows but me! I
No - bod-y knows what I know, No - bod-y knows but me! It's

hunt-ed a-round and a-round a - bout To find the__ se-cret, and found it out.
high - up - high in an ap - ple tree, And snug and__safe as a nest can be.

No - bod-y knows what I____ know,____ No - bod-y knows but me!
No - bod-y knows what we____ know— The Mo-ther__ bird and me!

Feather or Fur

John Becker (adapted)

Marlys Swinger

Gently

pp

When you watch for Feath-er or fur, Feath-er or fur, Feath-er or fur,

When you watch for Feath-er or fur, Do not stir, Do not stir. Feath-er or fur Come

crawl-ing, Creep-ing, Feath-er or fur Come soft-ly Peep-ing, Some by night And

some by day. Most come gen-tly, All come soft-ly; Do not scare A friend a-way.

The Winter Now Is Over

Translated by
Katherine F. Rohrbough

Italian-Swiss Folk Song

Gaily

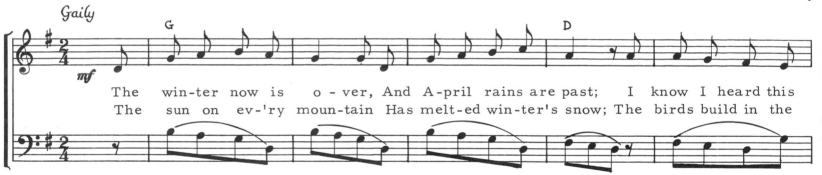

The win-ter now is o-ver, And A-pril rains are past; I know I heard this
The sun on ev-'ry moun-tain Has melt-ed win-ter's snow; The birds build in the

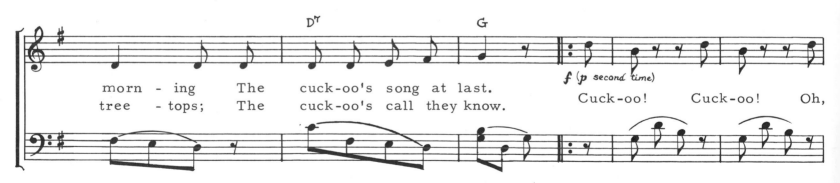

morn - ing The cuck-oo's song at last.
tree - tops; The cuck-oo's call they know.

Cuck-oo! Cuck-oo! Oh,

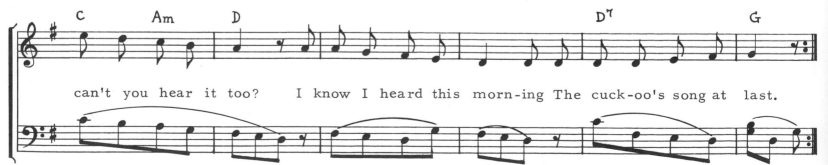

can't you hear it too? I know I heard this morn-ing The cuck-oo's song at last.

18

Dandelion

Scottish Folk Verse

Marlys Swinger

Lightly

I'm a hap-py lit-tle thing, Al-ways com-ing with the spring; In the
Lit-tle chil-dren, when you pass Light-ly on the ten-der grass, Skip a-

mead-ows green I'm found, Peep-ing just a-bove the ground, And my stalk is cov-ered
bout but do not tread On my small and low-ly head. I'm the flow'r that comes to

flat With a fuz-zy, yel-low hat.
say, "Win-ter - time has gone a - way."

Wise Johnny

Edwina Fallis

Marlys Swinger

Lit - tle John - ny - jump - up said, "Now it must be spring,

I just saw a la - dy - bug And heard a rob - in sing."

White Coral Bells

2 Part Canon

White cor-al bells up-on a slen-der stalk, Lil - ies of the val-ley deck my gar-den walk.
Oh, don't you wish that you could hear them ring? That will happen on-ly when the fair-ies sing.

Crocuses

3 Part Round

Japanese Haiku by Jōsa
Translated by William N. Porter

Erika Hildel

The sun-rise tints the dew; The yel-low cro-cus-es are out, And I must pick a few.

Daffodillies

Words and Music by
A.W.I. Chitty

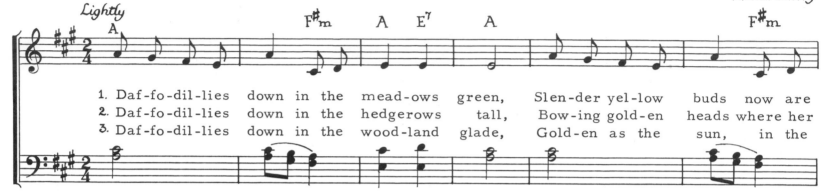

1. Daf-fo-dil-lies down in the mead-ows green, Slen-der yel-low buds now are
2. Daf-fo-dil-lies down in the hedgerows tall, Bow-ing gold-en heads where her
3. Daf-fo-dil-lies down in the wood-land glade, Gold-en as the sun, in the

droop-ing seen. Raise your trum-pets to the sky, For Spring, happy Spring is passing by.
foot-steps fall. Raise your trum-pets to the sky, For Spring, happy Spring is passing by.
deep, cool shade. Raise your trum-pets to the sky, For Spring, happy Spring is passing by.

Caterpillars

Aileen Fisher

George Burleson

Wonderingly

What do cat - er - pil-lars do? Noth-ing much but chew and chew. What do cat - er-

pil-lars know? Noth-ing much but how to grow. They just eat what by and by will

make them be a but-ter-fly, But that is more than I can do how-ev-er much I chew and chew.

A Happy Goodmorning

Ivy O. Eastwick

Marlys Swinger

Merrily

It is a hap-py morn-ing— there is blos-som on the trees, there's a
sin-gle dew-drop cling-ing like a rain-bow to a rose, and the

mer-ry rob-in sing-ing, there's a gold-en flight of bees, there's a
sun is bus-y shed-ding lit-tle freckles on Jon's nose. Oh, it

IS a hap-py morn-ing, there is joy in ev-'ry-thing, such a

good and hap-py morn-ing Jon has sim-ply GOT to sing.

24

On a Summer Morning
("When Over Sunlit Paths")

English lyrics by
Antonia Ridge

F. W. Möller

Cheerfully

1. When on a summer morn-ing, As I go on my way, And hear the brown bird
2. Oh, on a summer morn-ing, When sunlit shines the way, And bum-ble bees go
3. When on a summer morn-ing, The joyous swallows play, Down where the brook goes
4. Oh, lovely summer morn-ing, When I go wand'ring by, And hear the sweet birds

sing - ing, And black-bird whist-ling gay, And high the lark goes wing-ing And
hum-ming, And whis-p'ring corn-fields sway, And summer breezes mur-mur The
danc-ing, And sing-ing all the day, And high on hill the cur-lew Goes
sing-ing, A - way all sor-rows fly, And high my heart goes wing-ing So

calls from sky so blue, Then, oh, I must go sing-ing, Must go sing-ing, too!
qui - et for-est through, Then, oh, I must go humming, Must go humming, too!
whistling clear and true, Then, oh, I must go whistling, Must go whistling, too!
full of joy a - new, That oh, I must go sing-ing, Must go sing - ing, too!

26

Tra-la-la-la, Tra-la-la-la, Tra-la-la-la-la, Tra-la-la-la-la-la-la-la,
Zum-zum-zum-zum, Zum-zum-zum-zum, Zum-zum-zum, Zum-zum-zum-zum,
(Whistle) _____ _____ _____ _____
Tra-la-la-la, Tra-la-la-la, Tra-la-la-la-la, Tra-la-la-la-la-la-la-la,

Tra-la-la-la, Tra-la-la-la, Must go sing-ing, too!
Zum-zum-zum-zum, Zum-zum-zum-zum, Must go humming, too!
(Whistle) _____ _____ Must go whist-ling, too!
Tra-la-la-la, Tra-la-la-la, Must go sing-ing, too!

The Little Tune

Rose Fyleman

Marlys Swinger

He played his lit-tle tune One sum-mer af-ter-noon, And on the grass-y
He played his lit-tle tune Be - neath the yel-low moon; So sweet it was, so

hill The ve-ry breeze was still, While ev-'ry but-ter-cup Looked up—looked up.
light, That (oh, the dar-ling sight) The bun-nies all drew near To hear — to hear.

Little Wind

Kate Greenaway
Gently

Marlys Swinger

*Flute or recorder descant

Lit-tle wind, blow on the hill-top, Lit-tle wind, blow down the plain;

Lit-tle wind, blow up the sun-shine, Lit-tle wind, blow off the rain.

Off to the Sea

Words and Music by
Klaus Barth

With jollity

1. We are off, we are off To the sea, to the sea, To the roll - ing, rock-ing sea! Let us speed a-long the way, We must reach the coast to-day, And there should be no de - lay! For we are go - ing to the sea fi-nal-ly, With hap-py song and jol - li - ty!

2. We are off, we are off To the sea, to the sea, To the roll - ing, rock-ing sea! If the sky is o-ver-cast, If the rain beats down so fast, Yet the sun comes out at last! For we are go - ing to the sea fi-nal-ly, With hap-py song and jol - li - ty!

3. We are off, we are off To the sea, to the sea, To the roll - ing, rock-ing sea! Our ja-lop - y dash-es on, Watch the road and don't go wrong, Step on the gas and sing a song! For we are go - ing to the sea fi-nal-ly, With hap-py song and jol - li - ty!

4. We are off, we are off To the sea, to the sea, To the roll - ing, rock-ing sea! Just a mile and 'round the bend, Here the jour-ney has an end, For the sea, the sea, my friend! For we have reached the roll - ing sea fi-nal-ly, With hap-py song and jol - li - ty!

On Silver Sands

Ivy O. Eastwick

Marlys Swinger

Smoothly

Come for a run by the sil-ver sea, come in the sun-light with

me, with me. The sands are sil-ver be-neath the sky— more

sil-ver a-bove them the sea-birds fly. Let us go run-ning a-

way to-geth-er all in the spray-fly-ing, wind-sigh-ing weath-er.

Three Little Puffins

Eleanor Farjeon   Marlys Swinger

Frolicsome

Three lit-tle puf-fins Were par-tial to muf-fins, As par-tial as par-tial can be.___ They would-n't eat nuf-fin But hot but-tered muf-fin For breakfast and din-ner and tea.___ Pant-in' and puff-in' And chew-in' and chuff-in' They just went on stuffin', dear me!___ Till the three lit-tle puf-fins Were chockful of muffins And puff-y as puff-y can be, All three Were puffy as puffy can be.

Cotton Needs A-Pickin'

Southern Folk Song

Rhythmic

Cot-ton needs a-pick-in' so bad,—

Cot-ton needs a-pick-in' so bad,— Cot-ton needs a-pick-in' so bad,— Gon-na

pick all o-ver this field. We planted this cot-ton in A-pril—— On the full of the
Hur-ry up, hur-ry up, chil-dren, Pick-in' should-a been

moon. We've had a hot, dry sum-mer, That's why it o-pened so soon.
done. This weath-er looks so cloud-y,— I think it's go-in' to storm.

34

I Pick Up My Hoe

Jamaican Folk Song

Syncopated

I pick up my hoe and I go, I pick up my hoe and I go-o-o, Come
I hoe where the young cot-ton grow, I hoe where the young cot-ton grow-ow-ow, O

with me and help hoe a row, And we'll hoe and we'll hoe and we'll hoe.
help hoe a young cot-ton row, And we'll hoe and we'll hoe and we'll hoe.

The Thunder Storm
("Rhyme")

Elizabeth Coatsworth   Vonnie Burleson

Gustily

I like to see a thun-der storm, A dun-der storm, A blun-der storm, I
I like to hear a thun-der storm, A plun-der storm, A won-der storm, Roar

like to see it, black and slow, Come stum-bling down the hills.
loud-ly at our lit-tle house And shake the win-dow sills!

36

In the Rain

Harvey W. Loomis
Rollicking

Woodcrest Community

1. Wa-ter in the gut-ter,— Wa-ter in the street, Wa-ter, wa-ter, wa-ter,
2. What a lot of black— um-brel-las go-ing by! Wa-ter, wa-ter, wa-ter,
3. Ev - 'ry-one is sop-py,— sop - py, sop-py wet. Wa-ter, wa-ter, wa-ter,

wet-ting people's feet. Oh, such a rain! But we won't com-plain.
drip-ping from the sky. Oh, how it pours! I'm glad we're out-doors.
pelt-ing hard-er yet. Oh, such big drops! Let's stay till it stops.

I Planted My Wheat

Translated from the German

From the Sudetenland

1. I plant-ed my wheat on the moun-tain-side, moun-tain-side; Down came the
2. Oh,___ Wild Wind, I would ask of you, ask of you, Please let my
3. When all my mon-ey is spent and gone, spent and gone, Twigs I will
4. Then I will bind them and make new brooms, make new brooms; Sure-ly I'll
5. Then I'll go sing - ing through the town, through the town, Walk-ing the

wind, blew it far and wide, far and wide, Down came the wind, blew it far and wide.
wheat on the moun-tain grow, moun-tain grow, Please let my wheat on the moun-tain grow!
cut___ and car-ry home, car-ry home, Twigs I will cut___ and car-ry home.
earn___ some mon-ey soon, mon-ey soon, Sure-ly I'll earn___ some mon-ey soon.
streets___ all up and down, up and down, "Peo-ple, come buy___ the brooms I've bound!"

Sweet Potatoes

English by
Harvey W. Loomis

Just for fun!

Creole Folk Song
Counter Melody by Hector Spaulding

1. Soon ez we-all cook swee' pe-ta-tehs, swee' pe-ta-tehs, swee' pe-ta-tehs,
2. Soon ez sup-per's et, Mam-my hol-lehs, Mam-my hol-lehs, Mam-my hol-lehs,
3. Soon's we tech our haids to de peel-lo, to de peel-lo, to de peel-lo,
4. Soon's de roos-ter crow in de mo'-nin', in de mo'-nin', in de mo'-nin',

Roo, roo, roo, roo, hoo, hoo, Sing ho-ke-dink-um!

Soon ez we-all cook swee' pe-ta-tehs, Eat 'em right straight up!
Soon ez sup-per's et Mam-my hol-lehs, "Git a-long to baid!"
Soon's we tech our haids to de peel-lo, Go to sleep right smart!
Soon's de roos-ter crow in de mo'-nin', Got-ta wash our face!

Roo, roo, roo, roo, hoo, hoo, hoo, hoo!

40

Summer Fun

Woodcrest School Children

German Folk Tune

With vigor

1. In summer when the sky is blue And there's sunny weath-er, We'll take our suits and
2. We climb the rocks, we turn a-round, Stand-ing there for-ev-er. Some jump in, and
3. All af-ter-noon we swim and dive Till we're cold and freezing, And one by one we

get in the bus, Boys and girls to-geth-er. Off to *Kaat-ers-kill we go,
some dive down, Some have cour-age nev-er. One-two-three—and off we go
strag-gle out, Sput-ter-ing and sneez-ing. Then at last toward home we turn,

Jump right in! O - ho! ho! ho! Laugh-ing all to - geth-er, Laughing all to-geth-er.
To the wa-ter down be - low, Splash-ing all to - geth-er, Splashing all to-geth-er.
Fa-ces red and shoul-ders burned, Mer-ri-ly we're singing, Mer-ri-ly we're singing.

* You may wish to substitute your favorite swimming place for "Kaaterskill."

Blue Cheese
("Yodel With Me")

English Lyrics by Josef Marais

Swiss Folk Song

1. My ma-ma once gave me some blue cheese to eat; She thought that to
2. Our clock has two hands and they're both the same size; When I tell the
3. I once saw a beau-ti-ful red but-ter-fly; It sat on a
4. Our bath-tub is big and the fau-cets are old; I turn on the

me it would be such a treat, But I sim-ply climbed to the top of the
time, I get such a sur-prise. At quar-ter past one it's so fun-ny for
rose-bush, a lit-tle too high. I swung with my net at that but-ter-fly
hot and the wa-ter is cold. But I know those fau-cets, I know what is

house And gave the blue cheese to the mouse, mouse, mouse.
me To know it's five min-utes past three, three, three.
red, And there in the net was my head, head, head.
what: I turn on the cold and it's hot, hot, hot.

*Tri - tul - ja

i - der-i tri-tul-ja i, Tri-tul-ja i-der-i tri-tul-ja i, -o. _____

* Pronounced: Tree-tool-ya-ee-der-ee

"Yodel with Me" Words and Music by Josef Marais
© 1952. Fideree Music Corporation. Used by permission.

Over the Meadows

English Lyrics by
Augustus D. Zanzig

Czech Folk Tune

With a lilt

O - ver the mead-ows green and wide, Blooming in the sun-light,
Sweet is the air with new-mown hay, Cool-ing in the twi-light,

Blooming in the sun - light, O - ver the meadows green and wide, Off we go a-roam-ing
Cool-ing in the twi - light, Sweet is the air with new-mown hay, As we homeward go at

side by side. (Hey!)
close of day. (Hey!) Stream-lets down mountains go, Pure from the win-ter's snow,

Join-ing they swift-ly go, Sing-ing of life so free. Stream-lets down mountains go,

Pure from the win-ter's snow,   Join-ing, they swift-ly go,   Call-ing   to   me!

The Puppy Dog Song

Words and Music by the
* Plough Boys

Syncopated

1. Oh, Ma-ma, look! See what I've found — A cute lit-tle pup-py dog play-ing a-round! With a nice shin-y coat___ that is so soft and clean, It looks like va-nil-la and choc-'late ice cream.

2. Oh, Ma-ma, look! See what she's doing — She's got my best sock___ and now she is chewing! Give it back to me, pup-py, now___ don't look so sad, You can have this old pant-leg that was from my Dad.

3. Oh, Ma-ma, look! See when I eat, With sad wish-ing eyes___ she sits at my feet! With her long fur-ry hair___ that is all in a muddle, Can I have her to keep,___ she's so nice to cuddle!

*The Plough Publishing House book-binders.

47

Trot Along

Just loping along

Words and Music by
Marlys Swinger

Trot a - long, my lit - tle po-ny, Trot a-long, my dap-ple-gray; There's a warm sta-ble wait-in' Filled with sweet-smell-in' hay. We've been ridin', we've been rop-in', We've been on the range all day; Trot a-long, my lit-tle po-ny, Trot a-long, my dap-ple-gray. We start-ed off at sun-rise, We nev-er stopped to rest, And

48

now the sun has slipped behind The moun-tains in the west. Trav-el on to your sta-ble With its

sweet smell-in' hay; Trot a - long, my lit-tle po-ny, Trot a-long, my dap-ple-gray.

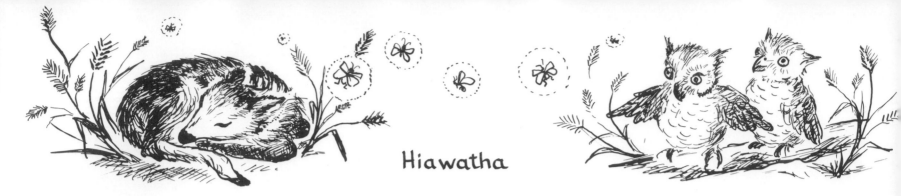

Hiawatha

Longfellow

H. A. Donald

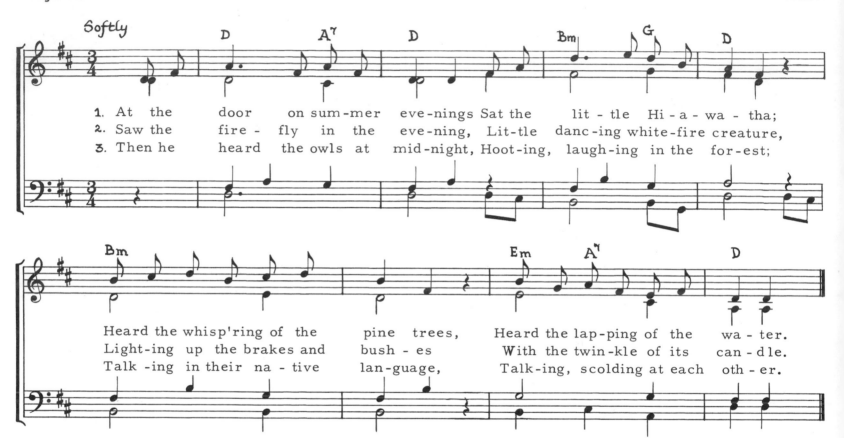

Softly

1. At the door on sum-mer eve-nings Sat the lit-tle Hi-a-wa-tha;
2. Saw the fire-fly in the eve-ning, Lit-tle danc-ing white-fire creature,
3. Then he heard the owls at mid-night, Hoot-ing, laugh-ing in the for-est;

Heard the whisp'ring of the pine trees, Heard the lap-ping of the wa-ter.
Light-ing up the brakes and bush-es With the twin-kle of its can-dle.
Talk-ing in their na-tive lan-guage, Talk-ing, scolding at each oth-er.

4. Then the little Hiawatha
Learned of every bird its language,
Where they built their nests in summer,
Where they hid themselves in winter.

5. Then of beasts he learned their language,
Learned their names and all their secrets,
Talked with them whene'er he met them,
Called them "Hiawatha's Brothers."

Land of the Silver Birch

With a steady rhythm

Canadian Folk Song

1. Land of the sil-ver birch, Home of the bea-ver, Land where the wild__ moose Wan-ders at will, Blue lake and rock-y shore, I will re-turn once more. Dip, dip, and swing a-long, Dip, dip, and swing.
2. Swift as the sil-ver fish — My ca-noe of birch bark, By might-y wa-ters Car-ried a-far, Blue lake and rock-y shore, I will re-turn once more. Dip, dip, and swing a-long, Dip, dip, and swing.
3. Down where the blue lake lies, I'll set my wig-wam; Un-der the shin-ing stars, I'll sing my song. Blue lake and rock-y shore, I will re-turn once more. Dip, dip, and swing a-long, Dip, dip, and swing.

Paddling My Canoe

Iroquois Song

Gay-o way-o wa-ji-ne__ he-ya he, Pad-dling my ca-noe, Gay-o way-o

wa-ji-ne,__ he - ya he-ya he, Pad-dling my ca-noe, pad-dling my ca-noe.

Drum

Come Out! Come Out!

Gladys Wolfe
from translation of
Kees Kooper

Dutch Canon

Come out! Come out to hear the call The gold-en bird is singing on the mall. Oh,

when you hear that sing-er grand, There is sum-mer in the land. Du-dle

du-dle, tweet, tweet, tweet, Du-dle du-dle sweet, sweet, sweet, Du-dle du-dle the song re-peat.

Remember September

May Justus

Marlys Swinger

Whimsically

Re - mem-ber Sep - tem-ber; Be - fore she said good-by   She told the youngest
Re - mem-ber Sep - tem-ber; Be - fore she went a - way   She taught the cricket

robins The way they ought to fly. A-round the mountain's shoul-der She spread a gyp-sy
fid-dlers The prop-er tunes to play. She gave a mod-est ma-ple A dress of red and

shawl, And sent a breeze a - mong the trees To sing a - bout the Fall.
gold, And showed a mouse a lit-tle house To keep him through the cold.

October and November

Clara Louise Kessler

Yugoslavian Folk Tune

Brightly

Man-y days are bright in Oc - to - ber; There is hap-pi-ness in the
When the frost is white on the mead - ows, When the winds of No-vem-ber

air. Red and yel - low leaves From the au-tumn trees Are drift-ing ev -'ry - where.
blow, Then the wild geese fly Toward the south-ern sky For soon we shall have snow.

From *Songs of Many Lands* of The World of Music series, copyright, 1936, 1943.
by Ginn and Company; copyright © renewed, 1964, by Mabelle Glenn and Earl
L. Baker. Used with permission.

Autumn Hiking Song

Vs. 1 - Unknown
Vs. 2 - Woodcrest Community

German Folk Tune

Briskly

The blue of the sky stretch-es high o'er the trees; The
The swim-ming at Kaat-ers-kill now is____ o-ver; The

leaves 'neath our feet make a car-pet be-low. The warm au-tumn air calls us
days in the bus have been fun for us all. The leaves now are turn-ing, the

out from our ease, And up from our la - bors we must go.
sky grows more blue, And out we must go in the cool bright fall.

Hi - o,____

hi - o, hi-o hi-o hi-o ho, hi - o, hi-o ho, hi - o. -o.

Come, Little Leaves

George Cooper

Unknown

Playfully

1. "Come, lit - tle leaves," said the Wind one day, "Come o'er the
2. Soon as the leaves heard the Wind's loud call, Down they came
3. Danc - ing and whirl - ing the lit-tle leaves went; Win - ter had

mead-ows with me and play; Put on your dress - es of
flut - ter-ing, one and all; O - ver the brown fields they
called them, and they were con - tent; Soon, fast a - sleep in their

red and gold For sum - mer is gone and the days grow cold."
danced and flew, A - sing - ing the glad lit - tle songs they knew.
earth - y beds, The snow laid a cov-er-let o-ver their heads.

Swinging Along

long the o-pen road,—   All   in the fall   of   the   year.

long the o-pen road,   All   in the fall   of   the   year.

Autumn Roundelay

English Lyrics by
Max T. Krone

Finnish Folk Song

Gently swaying

Here I sit and wait for you 'Neath the spreading branch-es. Cool the grass with
Fall is in the air to-day; Hear the wild geese cry - ing. Don't de - lay, come

shade and dew; Sun-light round me danc - es. Hei, lu - li-a li - a - la,
while you may; Snow will soon be fly - ing.

Loud my voice is ring - ing, Hei, lu - li-a li - a - la, Songs to you I'm sing - ing.

* Optional as a two-part canon.

62

The Willow's Lullaby

Translated from the Swedish

Z. Topelius

Smoothly

Sleep, thou lit-tle wil-low tree, Through the win-ter weath-er, With the blue-bell
Gen-tle winds shall cra-dle thee, And the sun watch o'er thee, Till the spring shall

and the rose, With the birch and heath-er. Wait un-til the sun is bright And the dog-wood
make the flow'rs Bow their heads be-fore thee. Then put off your silver down: Don your shining

blossoms white. Sleep, thou lit-tle wil-low tree, Through the win-ter weath-er.
gold-en gown. Gen-tle winds shall cra-dle thee, And the sun watch o'er thee.

Hurry, Hurry, Hurry

Jack-o'-Lantern

German Folk Tune

Lois Holt

Cheerfully

Jack-o'-Lan-tern, Jack-o'-Lan-tern, You are such a fun-ny
You were once a yel-low pump-kin Grow-ing on a stur-dy

sight, As you sit there in the win-dow Look-ing out at the night.
vine. Now you are a Jack-o'-Lan-tern: See the can-dle-light shine.

Wind, Wind, Blowing

2-part Canon

Paula Dehmel

At an easy walking pace

Gottfried Wolters

1. Wind, wind, blow-ing, The moon, it is not show-ing. The moon has gone a-
2. Stars, stars, glim-mer, The moon is just a shim-mer. She has a sick-le
3. Moon, bright-er grow-ing, Your love-ly rays now throw-ing. They are of fin-est

way so far To catch a lit-tle shoot-ing star. Wind, wind, blow-ing, The
in her hand To cut the grass in heav-en's land. Stars, stars, glim-mer, The
sil-ver sand— You sow it o-ver sea and land. Moon, brighter grow-ing, Your

moon, it is not show-ing.
moon is just a shim-mer.
love-ly rays now throw-ing.

4. Moon, shine brighter,
Our lanterns are still lighter.
They light our pathway through the night
With lovely warm and glowing light.
Moon, shine brighter,
Our lanterns are still lighter.

"Wind, Wind, sause" from *Das singende Jahr*, used by permission of Möseler Verlag, Wolfenbüttel and Zürich.
Translated from the German by the Society of Brothers. Vs. 4 added.

High and Blue the Sky

Paraphrase of the Chinese
With a steady rhythm

Chinese Folk Song

High and blue the sky;   Trees are ve-ry tall;   Wild geese fly-ing seem so
Clear and dark the night;   Stars are ve-ry bright;   Lan-terns shin-ing seem so

small.   See, on si-lent wings in flocks they go,
small.   See, in sin-gle file we walk a-long,

Nev-er part-ing from the sin-gle row. We go through the land,
Sing-ing joy-ful-ly our lan-tern song. We go through the land,

Like the wild geese band: Bro-thers in the flight are we.
Like the wild geese band: Bro-thers of one light are we.

Down with Darkness
("Banou Choshech Legaresh")

S. Levi-Tanai
Strongly accented

E. Amiran

Down with dark-ness, up with light; Up with sun-shine, down with night.
Down with dark-ness, up with light; Up with sun-shine, down with night.

Each of us is one small light, But to-geth-er we shine bright.
Small lights gath-er one by one, Drive out dark till night is done.

Go a-way, dark-est, black-est night, Go a-way, give way to light!
Go a-way, dark-est, black-est night, Go a-way, give way to light!

Translated by Tom Glazer. Verse 2 added.

With a Lantern in the Hand

Eberhard Arnold
Translated from the German

Marianne Zimmermann

Gently swinging

With a lan-tern in the hand,
With a lan-tern in the hand,

Joy-ful-ly go through the land. One to the right, One to the left: We must show to
Joy-ful-ly go through the land. One to the right, One to the left: We must show to

all the light! Through-out the land! As one band! Light____ in hand!
all the light! Up through the land! Up through the land! Light____ in hand!

Harvest Song

Unknown

Marlys Swinger

Rollicking

The boughs do shake and the bells do ring, So mer-ri-ly comes our har-vest in, Our

har-vest in, our har-vest in, So mer-ri-ly comes our har-vest in.

We have ploughed and we have sowed, We have reaped and we have mowed,

We have brought home ev-'ry load, Hip, hip, hip, our har-vest home! _____ The

Potato Harvest

English Lyrics by
Constance Rumbough

Traditional from
White Russia

Gay, with vigorous rhythm

1. Dig, oh dig with pick and spade, And fer-ret out___where spuds are laid:
2. Boil them, bake them, fry them, stew them, Roast them, scallop them, praise them too:
3. Har-vest now is gath-ered in; Po-ta-toes good___ fill ev-'ry bin;

Dig them, fling them in your sack, And toss it la-den on your back.
Bet-ter food than all your frills, And they will help___us pay our bills.
Down the mead-ow in a ring, Now dance we mer-ri-ly as we sing!

Tum tum tum tee tee tum tum tum, Tum tum tum tee tee tum tum tum tee tee,

Tum tum tum tee tee tum tum tum, Tum tum tum tum tum tee tee tum.

Sung at Harvest Time

English Version by
Christine Turner Curtis

Inca Melody

With a steady rhythm

Come, my sisters, come, my brothers, At the sounding of the horn; On the hillsides,
Praise to Thee, O might-y In-ti, For the barley and the cane! In the wheat fields,

on the moun-tains, Har-vest we the yellow corn. Gold-en shines our Father Sun;
in the corn fields, Har-vest we the yellow grain. Soft-ly blows the au-tumn wind;

Silver shines our Mother Moon; Sickles flashing, fill your baskets, Reaping in the yellow noon.
Gently wave the silken leaves; Reapers singing, press we onward, Tying up the yellow sheaves.

Out in the Meadows

Danish Folk Song

Lively

Out in the meadows the grain has been cra-dled, Rye and wheat are stacked and soon the
Soon we shall har-vest the corn which is rip-ened; Gen-'rous-ly it pays the faith-ful

Autumn Song

Phyllis McGinley

Marlys Swinger

Gaily

D   A⁷   D

1. When the swal-lows   Quit the hol-lows   And the wild goose fol-lows   af - ter,
2. Oh, the fall-ing   Leaves are call-ing,   And we want to tum-ble   af - ter.
3. When the spi - cy   Pines are i - cy   And the North Wind shakes the raf - ter,

A   A⁷   D

Come! in-to the woods we'll has - ten,   Come! in-to the woods we'll has - ten, There to
Come! in-to the woods we'll has - ten,   Come! in-to the woods we'll has - ten, There to
Come! in-to the woods we'll has - ten,   Come! in-to the woods we'll has - ten, Welcome

A⁷   D

greet the fall with laugh-ter.
greet the fall with laugh-ter.
win - ter in with laugh-ter.

Words of vs. 1 and 3 paraphrased from the German by Phyllis McGinley.
From *Music Highways and Byways*, copyright, 1936, by Silver Burdett
Company. Reprinted by permission of the publisher. Verse 2 added by
Woodcrest Community.

I Like Winter

Words and Music
Lois Lenski

Arrangement by
Clyde Robert Bulla

I like win-ter, I like snow,
I can make a snow-man fat,

I like i-cy winds that blow. I like snow-flakes, oh so light, Mak-ing all the
Eyes and nose and fun-ny hat. I can squeeze a snow-ball tight. Throw it in a

ground so white. I like slid-ing down the hill, I like tum-bling in a spill!
snow-ball fight. I can skate and slip and slide — Ice is thick, the pond is wide.

Oh, ho! sea-sons come and sea-sons go. I like win-ter, I like snow.

Winter Fun

Nancy Byrd Turner

Marlys Swinger

Jolly

Bring your sleds to the coast-ing hill: Firm and fine the snow is ly-ing,
Bring your skates, it is crisp and cold, Sun shines bright, and the pond is wait-ing.

Glis-t'ning white in the win-ter chill! Haul them up with a right good will.
All join hands in a mer-ry row, One, two, three and a-way we go.

Yours is yel-low and mine is blue. All get set as we count, one, two,
Hear the ice, how it hums a song, Keen, clear song as we skim a-long,

Fling face down with a one, two, three, Off like birds on the wing are we!
For-ward, swift in the nip-ping air, Feet in time and the wind set fair.

Winter Night

Mary Frances Butts

Marlys Swinger

Stormy

1. Blow, Wind,— blow! Drift the fly-ing snow! Send it twirl-ing, whirl-ing o-ver-head!— There's a bed-room in a tree Where, as snug as snug can be, The squir-rel nests with-in his co-sy bed.—

2. Shriek, Wind,— shriek! Make the branch-es creak! Bat-tle with the boughs till break of day!— In a snow-cave warm and tight, Through the i-cy win-ter night, The rab-bit sleeps the peace-ful hours a-way.—

3. Call, Wind,— call, In en-try and in hall, Straight from off the moun-tain white and wild!— Soft-ly purrs the pus-sy-cat On her lit-tle fluf-fy mat, And near her nest-les close her fur-ry child.—

4. Scold, Wind,— scold, So bit-ter and so bold! Shake the win-dows with your tap, tap, tap!— With his half-shut dream-y eyes, There the drow-sy ba-by lies So close-ly cud-dled in his mo-ther's lap.—

Smoothly

The Mitten Song

Marie Louise Allen

Marlys Swinger

Merrily

"Thumbs in the thumb-place, Fingers all together!" This is the song We sing in mitten-weather.

When it is cold, It doesn't matter whether Mit-tens are wool Or made of finest leather.

This is the song We sing in mitten-weather: "Thumbs in the thumb-place, Fingers all together!"

82

Icicles

Woodcrest Preschool

Woodcrest Community

I like i-ci-cles long and straight.

Lick them, lick them Be-fore it's too late!

You should pick The i-ci-cles quick Be-

fore the sun Makes them all run.

The Sleds Go Zooming

4 Part Round

Woodcrest Preschool

Debra Swinger

The sleds go zoom - - ing down the hill, But at the bot - tom they stand still. Then we must pull them up and up, And we'll stay warm if we don't stop.

Coasting Song

Rose Miles

Swedish Folk Tune

Gaily

Skies are blue as blue can be, So bring your sleds and come with me. O'er the drift-ed,
Swift as swal-lows we will sweep A-down the hill-side long and steep, Dart-ing to the

gleam-ing snow The hap-py breez-es light-ly blow. Heigh-ho! Loud we cry!
plain be-low With laugh-ing fac-es all a-glow. Heigh-ho! Loud we cry!

Heigh - ho! Dart-ing by. Heigh - ho! See us fly! Down we go!
Heigh - ho! Dart-ing by. Heigh - ho! See us fly! Down we go!

From *Juvenile Music* of the Music Education Series, copyright, 1923, by Ginn and Company. Used with permission.

Jack Frost

Cecily Pike

Ivor R. Davies

Crisply

Look out! look out! Jack Frost is a-bout! He's af-ter our fin-gers and toes;___ And
A - cross the grass He'll mer-ri-ly pass And change all its greenness to white,___Then

all through the night The gay lit-tle sprite Is work-ing when no-bod-y knows.___ He'll
home he will go And laugh,"Ho! ho! ho! What fun I have had in the night."___

climb each tree, So nim-ble is he, His sil-ver-y pow-der he'll shake;___ To

win-dows he'll creep And while we're asleep, Such won-der-ful pic-tures he'll make.___

Little Snowflake

Translated

German Folk Song

Very Lightly

1. Lit - tle snow - flake, light snow - flake, In your white skirt float
2. Come and stay on my win - dow Like a love - ly, bright
3. Lit - tle snow - flake, come cov - er All the flow - ers with

down; From the clouds you come drift-ing To us here on the ground.
star; Draw some flow - ers and ferns too — Bring us joy from a - far.
snow So they'll sleep warm and safe - ly Till the spring breez-es blow.

O Fir Tree Tall

Translated

German Folk Song

Thoughtfully

1. O fir tree tall! O fir tree tall! Your
2. When all the trees a-round___ us In
3. "Why should I not grow tall and green? This
4. "But One there is who cares for me, That

boughs are ev - er green. In
si - lent sad - ness stand, You
I can sure - ly do. I
is the God of all. He

win - ter, in sum - mer, The
are so green, dear fir tree, In
have no mo-ther or fa - ther To
lets me grow and in - crease, Grow

same hue can be seen.
white and win - try land.
care for me, 'tis true.
slen-der, green, and tall."

The Snowman

Translated from the German

Marianne Zimmermann

1. Yo - ho, yo - ho, yo - ho! There stands a man of snow!
2. He has a splen - did hat, It fits him just like that!
3. But when the sun is high, The snow-man starts to cry.
4. And when warm breez - es blow, The fat snow-man must go.

Heis - sa vic - tor - i - a, There stands a man of snow.
Heis - sa vic - tor - i - a, It fits him just like that.
Heis - sa vic - tor - i - a, The snow-man starts to cry.
Heis - sa vic - tor - i - a, The fat snow-man must go.

5. Now children, come and see!
   Our snowman — gone is he!
   Heissa victoria,
   Our snowman — gone is he!

January and February

Jane B. Walters

German Folk Tune

Energetically

When Jan-u-ar-y days are here, The air is crisp, the sky is clear, Come
When Feb-ru-ar-y north winds blow, Lake, hill, and road are heaped with snow, Come

join our out-door play,__ Come join our out-door play. For o'er the ice we're glid-ing, Or
join our in-door play,__ Come join our in-door play. Like lit-tle gob-lins hop-ping, The

down the hill we're slid-ing, Or in a bob-sled rid-ing In Jan-u-ar-y days.__
feath-ery corn is pop-ping, In salt-y pan soon drop-ping In Feb-ru-ar-y days.__

Popcorn Song

Nancy Byrd Turner

Marlys Swinger

Jolly

1. Sing a song of pop-corn When the snow-storms rage:___ Fif-ty lit-tle
2. Sing a song of pop-corn In the fire - light;___ Fif-ty lit-tle
3. Sing a song of pop-corn; Done the frol- ick - ing;___ Fif-ty lit-tle

brown men Put in - to a cage.__ Shake them till they laugh and leap
fai - ries Robed in fleec - y white.__ Through the shin-ing wires__ see
fai - ries Strung up - on a string.__ Cool and hap - py, hand in hand,

Crowd-ing to the top;___ Watch them burst their lit-tle coats, Pop! Pop! Pop!___
How they skip and prance To the mu - sic of the flames, Dance! Dance! Dance!
Sug-ar-span-gled, fair:___ Is - n't that a neck-lace fit for An-y child to wear?

Winter-Walk

Ivy O. Eastwick

Marlys Swinger

Peacefully

Rose-red is the eve-ning sky, milk-white is the snow,

let's go on our eve-ning walk — do, do let us go. To-

mor-row the sky may be dull and grey, to-mor-row the snow may be gone, so

let us go on a Win-ter's walk in the last rays of the sun.

From *In and Out the Windows*, © 1969 by The Plough Publishing House.

Willows in the Snow

(Japanese Haiku)

Tsūrū
Translated by William N. Porter

Erika Hildel

The wil-lows hanging low, The wil-lows hanging low

Shake, shake, shake from their long and trailing skirts The fresh-ly fall - en snow.

* Optional as a round

All That Hath Life and Breath

Psalm 150:6

J. C. Blumhardt

All that hath life and breath, Life and breath,
Al - les, was O - dem hat, O - dem hat,

Praise the Lord! Praise the Lord,
Lo - be den Herrn! Lo - be den Herrn,

Hal - le - lu-jah, Hal - le - lu-jah!
Hal - le - lu-jah, Hal - le - lu-jah!

My New Little Sister

Word ideas by a
4-year-old child

Marlys Swinger

Simple and childlike

My new lit-tle sis-ter is ti-ny and small, She can-not play with us at all.
And sometimes my new lit-tle sister's a-sleep, And sometimes she smiles or she cries.

Her two lit-tle hands and her two lit-tle feet Are just right for her, they're so small.
My mommy can hold her, but I'll have to wait, And when she's much bigger we'll play.

But she cannot stand up and she cannot sit Be-cause she's so new and so small.
But now since she's little and ti-ny and sweet, I'll sing to her till she's a-sleep.

At the Gate of Heaven

Mexican Folk Song

Gently

At the gate of Heav'n lit-tle shoes they are giv-ing For the lit-tle
God will bless the chil-dren so peace-ful-ly sleep-ing, God will help the

bare-foot-ed an-gels there liv-ing. Slum-ber, my ba-by,
mo-thers whose love they are keep-ing. Slum-ber, my ba-by,

Slum-ber, my ba-by, Slum-ber, my ba-by, ar-ru, ar-ru.

This Is Your Birthday

Words and Music by Woodcrest Preschool

This is your birth-day, Your ve-ry spe-cial hap-py day, With lots of fun And a "stick-y - bun" For break - fast. A can-dle to blow And some more in a row, Lots of can-dy to share And new clothes to wear, With sur-pris-es all day, You'll be mer-ry and gay On your birth - day.

Oh, Birthdays Are Fun

Words and Music by
Woodcrest High School Group

With a gay lilt

Oh, birth-days are fun through-out the year — In rain or in shine they al-ways bring cheer. The leaves of au-tumn, the flow-ers of spring, White snow-flakes of win-ter, they all seem to sing, "Hap-py birth-day, hap-py birth-day, Hap-py birth-day greetings we bring." "Hap-py bring."

Dicky-bird Birthday Song

Maria Berchtenbreiter
Translated from the German

Leonore Pfund

Cheerfully

Our (Pe-ter's) birth-day is to-day, And all good wish-es come his way. A dick-y-bird pipes up to say, "O birth-day child, be glad and gay, O birth-day child, O birth-day child, Be glad and gay."

Today Is Your Birthday

Tom Glazer

Israeli Melody adapted by
Tom Glazer

To - day is your birthday, To - day is your birthday, To - day is a very special day for you. To - day for you. To - day is your fun day, Your

dance-in-the-sun day, To - day is a ve-ry special day for you. Oh, it's very pleasant To

* Original words : big number-one day.

o - pen a pres - ent. To - day is a mir-a-cle, a dream come true.

Nibble, Nibble, Nibble

Margaret Wise Brown

Marlys Swinger

Gaily

1. Nibble, nibble, nibble goes the mouse in my heart,
2. Lippity, lippity, clip goes the rabbit in my heart,
3. Flippity, flippity, flop goes the fish in my heart,
4. Biff, bang, bang goes the hammer in my heart,

Nibble, nibble, nibble goes the mouse in my heart,
Lippity, lippity, clip goes the rabbit in my heart,
Flippity, flippity, flop goes the fish in my heart,
Biff, bang, bang goes the hammer in my heart,

5. Drum, drum, drum goes the drum in my heart,
Drum, drum, drum goes the drum in my heart,
Drum, drum, drum goes the drum in my heart,
And the drum in my heart is you.

Nibble, nibble, nibble goes the mouse in my heart, And the
Lippity, lippity, clip goes the rabbit in my heart, And the
Flippity, flippity, flop goes the fish in my heart, And the
Biff, bang, bang goes the hammer in my heart, And the

mouse in my heart is you.
rabbit in my heart is you.
fish in my heart is you.
hammer in my heart is you.

* 6. Softly now beats the beat of my heart,
Softly now beats the beat of my heart,
Softly now beats the beat of my heart
All for the love of you.

※Children will enjoy making up their own verses.

Time for Rabbits

Aileen Fisher

Marlys Swinger

Lightly

"Look!" says the cat-kin in its gray hat-kin. "Look!" say the larks and spar-rows. "The
"Look!" wind is humming. "Easter is coming. Hear how the brook-let rush-es. It's

pas-ture is stir-ring, the wil-lows are pur-ring, and sun-light is shoot-ing its ar-rows."
time for the rab-bits with Eas-ter-egg hab-its to get out their paints and brush-es."

Lippity-Lop

Words and Music by
Margaret Fletcher
Margaret Denison

Lip-pi-ty-lop, lip-pi-ty-lop, Here comes a bun-ny, hip-pi-ty-hop, With

ears so tall and tail so small, Lip-pi-ty, lip-pi-ty, lop.—(lop, lop.)

(2nd time)

Fine

He sits up straight and wig-gles his ears At ev-'ry sound he hears,___ Then

scam-pers a-way as fast as he can And sud-den-ly dis-ap-pears. Oh!

D.C.

White Clouds

Words and Music by
Sylvia Beels

Joyfully

1. White clouds sail-ing in the wind - y sky, What is your mes-sage as you go float-ing by? "Joy to the peo-ple, joy and hope we bring For Je-sus Christ is ris - en! Ris - en! Our Lord and King!"
2. Wild geese flock-ing t'ward the glow - ing dawn, What are you shout-ing on this bright Eas-ter morn? "Joy to the peo-ple, joy and hope we bring For Je-sus Christ is ris - en! Ris - en! Our Lord and King!"
3. Flow'rs of the mead-ows bloom-ing fair a-mid the grass, What are you say - ing as the peo-ple pass? "Joy to the peo-ple, joy and hope we bring For Je-sus Christ is ris - en! Ris - en! Our Lord and King!"
4. Bro - thers and sis - ters and chil-dren in a throng, Let earth be ring - ing with your joy-ful song: "Joy to the peo-ple, joy and hope we bring For Je-sus Christ is ris - en! Ris - en! Our Lord and King!"

At Easter-time

Frederick A. Jackson

H. v. Müller

At Eas-ter-time the li-lies fair And love-ly flow'rs bloomed ev'ry-where. At
At Eas-ter-time the an-gels said That Christ had ris - en__ from the dead. At

Eas - ter-time, at__ Eas-ter-time, How glad the world at__ Eas-ter-time.
Eas - ter-time, at__ Eas-ter-time, How glad the world at__ Eas-ter-time.

110

Easter Eggs

English Lyrics by
Percy Dearmer

Russian Easter Song

Evenly

1. Eas-ter eggs! Eas-ter eggs! Give to him that begs! For
2. To the poor, o-pen door, something give from your store! For
3. Those who hoard can't af-ford — moth and rust their re-ward! For
4. Those who love free-ly give — long and well may they live! For
5. Eas-ter - tide, Eas-ter - tide comes and won't be de-nied, For

Christ the Lord is a-ris-en,____ is a-ris-en.____

Advent

Translated   German Folk Tune

Ad – vent! Advent! A   can-dle burns. Ad-vent! Advent! A   can-dle burns. First

one, then two, Then   three, then four, Then   stands the   Christ-child   At   the door.

Gloria!
2 Part Canon

Woodcrest Preschool   Debra Swinger

Glo – ri – a,   glo-ri – a,   Let us all now   joy-ful sing   Wel-come to   our

ba – by   King.   Glo – ri – a,   glo-ri – a,   Glo – ri – a,   glo – ri-a!

Come, Every Angel

Woodcrest Preschool

Marlys Swinger

Joyfully

1. Come, ev-'ry an-gel, to the stall, Make it read-y for Je-sus small.
2. In - to the man-ger, hay we bring, All for Je-sus, our lit - tle King—
3. Now we will hang the spark-ling stars So they shine both near and far—
4. Ev - 'ry-thing's read-y for our King! Joy-ful, joy-ful___ we will sing,

All of us car-ry can-dles bright That will make the sta-ble light.
Pil - low and sheets and blan-ket too, All for Je-sus,___ small and new.
Christ-mas chains and cook-ies too, All for Je-sus,___ small and new.
For He comes to earth this night And will make the dark world light.

La la la la, la la la la la, La la la la, la la la la la,

La la la la, la la la la la, La la la la, la la la la la.

The Birds

Translation from
The Oxford Book of Carols

Czech Carol

Tenderly

1. From out of a wood did a cuck-oo fly, Cuck-oo, He came to a
2. A pi-geon flew o-ver to Ga-li-lee, Vrer-croo, He strut-ted, and
3. A dove set-tled down up-on Na-za-reth, Tsu-croo, And ten-der-ly

man-ger with joy-ful cry, Cuck-oo; He hopped, he curt-sied, round he
cooed, and was full of glee, Vrer-croo, And showed, with jew-eled wings un-
chant-ed with all his breath, Tsu-croo: "O you," he cooed, "so good and

flew, And loud his ju-bi-la-tion grew, Cuck-oo, cuck-oo, cuck-oo.
furled, His joy that Christ was in the world, Vrer-croo, vrer-croo, vrer-croo.
true, My beau-ty do I give to you." Tsu-croo, tsu-croo, tsu-croo.

Ding Dong!

Translated

French Tune, 16th Century

Ding dong! Mer-ri-ly on high, In Heav'n the bells are ring - ing.
E'en so here be - low, Let all the bells be swing - ing,

Ding dong! Ve-ri-ly the sky Is riv'n with an - gels sing - ing.
And i - o, i - o, Hear all the peo - ple sing - ing!

Glo - - - - - - - - - - - - -

- - - - ri - a, Ho - san - na in ex - cel - sis.

O Come Little Children

Christoph von Schmid

J.A.P. Schulz

Joyfully, not too fast

1. O come lit-tle chil-dren, O come one and all, To Beth-le-hem has-ten, and to the cow's stall. We'll see what our Fa-ther this ho-li-est night Has sent to His chil-dren for joy and de-light.
2. O see in His cra-dle in star-light full bright, See here where now streams from a-bove a great light! A dear lit-tle ba-by, a heav-en-ly child, More love-ly than an-gels His smile sweet and mild.
3. See Ma-ry and Jo-seph a glad vi-gil keep, Where cra-dled in hay He lies soft-ly a-sleep. In awe see the shep-herds who kneel round the King; On high, an-gel choirs all their glad car-ols sing.
4. O kneel like the shep-herds and like them all pray; With hands gent-ly fold-ed, to God your thanks say. Then sing and be mer-ry—who would not re-joice? And join with the an-gels your heart and your voice.

Pat-a-pan

Bernard de la Monnoye
English lyrics A.D. Zanzig

French Carol

Steadily

1. Wil-lie, bring your lit-tle drum; Rob-in, take your flute
2. When the folk of oth-er days To the King of Kings
3. God and man to-day are one Like the sounding flute

Pan, pat-a-pan, pat-a-pan, pat-a-pan, pat-a-pan, pat-a-pan, pat-a-pan, pat-a-pan, (cont.)

and come: We'll be mer-ry as you play, Tu-re-lu-re-lu, pat-a-pat-a-
gave praise, On the flute and drum they'd play, Tu-re-lu-re-lu, pat-a-pat-a-
and drum, We'll be mer-ry as you play, Tu-re-lu-re-lu, pat-a-pat-a-

pan, We'll be mer-ry as you play, For a Christmas should be gay.___
pan, On the flute and drum they'd play, And their hearts were ver-y gay.___
pan, We'll be mer-ry as you play, For a Christmas should be gay.___

Under Bethlehem's Star

English Lyrics by
Mary Cochrane Vojáček

Czech Carol
Arranged by
Vilém Tauský

Very gaily

1. Un-der Beth-l'em's star so bright, Shepherds watched their flocks by night.
2. Came an an-gel tell-ing them, They must go to Beth-le-hem.
3. "Has-ten, has-ten," they did say, "Je-sus Christ you'll find that way."

Hy-dom, hy-dom, tid-li-dom, Hy-dom, hy-dom, tid-li-dom.

4. Sleeping in a manger bare
Lies the holy Child so fair.
Hy-dom, hy-dom, tid-li-dom,
Hy-dom, hy-dom, tid-li-dom.

5. Mary rocks Him tenderly,
Joseph sings a lullaby.
Hy-dom, hy-dom, tid-li-dom,
Hy-dom, hy-dom, tid-li-dom.

There's a Star in the East

Spiritual

mf

There's a star in the East on Christmas morn, Rise up, shepherd, and follow: It will
If you take good heed to the an-gel's word, Rise up, shepherd, and follow: You'll for-

lead to the place where the Sav-ior's born,___ Rise up, shep-herd, and fol-low!___
get your flock, you'll for - get your herd;___ Rise up, shep-herd, and fol-low!___

Leave your flocks and leave your lambs, Rise up, shep-herd, and fol-low,___

Leave your sheep and leave your rams, Rise up, shep-herd, and fol-low.___

Fol - low, fol - low, Rise up, shep-herd, and fol-low,___

Fol-low the star of Beth-le - hem,___ Rise up, shep-herd, and fol-low.

Rocking

Translation from
The Oxford Book of Carols

Czech Carol

Lit - tle Je - sus, sweet - ly sleep, do not stir; We will lend a_
Ma - ry's lit - tle ba - by, sleep, sweet - ly sleep, Sleep in com - fort,

coat of_ fur. We will rock you, rock you, rock you. We will rock you,
slum - ber deep; We will rock you, rock you, rock you. We will rock you,

rock you, rock you: See the fur to keep you warm, Snug - ly round your ti - ny form.
rock you, rock you: We will serve you all we can, Dar - ling, dar - ling lit - tle man.

The Lowly Stable

Translated

German Carol

1. See, there stands a— low-ly— sta-ble; A ho-ly light is burn-ing with-in.
2. O who's there in the low-ly— sta-ble? O may they just not freeze with cold.
3. With-in is Ma-ry, who wash-es the ba-by; The ba-by Je-sus she wash-es there. With-
4. The old man Jo-seph is in the— sta-ble; A love-ly long white beard has he. The

See, there stands a— low-ly— sta-ble; A ho-ly light is burn-ing with-in.
O who's there in the low-ly— sta-ble? O may they just not freeze with cold.
in is Ma-ry, who wash-es the ba-by; The ba-by Je-sus she wash-es there.
old man Jo-seph is in— the sta-ble; A love-ly long white beard has he.

5. He moves his foot and he rocks the cradle;
   He's rocking Jesus to and fro.
   He moves his foot and he rocks the cradle;
   He's rocking Jesus to and fro.

6. The donkey is breathing, the ox is blowing
   To keep the baby Jesus warm.
   The donkey is breathing, the ox is blowing
   To keep the baby Jesus warm.

Susani

Translation from the German by
Katherine F. Rohrbough

Kölner Gesangbuch 1623

Smoothly

1. From Heav - en high, bright an - gels, come! Ei - a! Ei - a!
2. His in - stru - ment let each one bring: Ei - a! Ei - a!
3. 'Tis heav'n-ly mu - sic you must play, Ei - a! Ei - a!
4. Sing peace to men the world a-round, Ei - a! Ei - a!

*Su-sa-ni, su-sa-ni, su - sa-ni! Come, sing and play, come, pipe and drum! Hal-
Su-sa-ni, su-sa-ni, su - sa-ni! A lute, a harp, sweet vi - o-lin! Hal-
Su-sa-ni, su-sa-ni, su - sa-ni! For Heav-en's Child is here to-day. Hal-
Su-sa-ni, su-sa-ni, su - sa-ni! Let praise to God for - e'er re-sound. Hal-

* Susani — "Rejoice ye," from the Hebrew.
  (Pronounced soo-zah-nee)

le - lu - ja! Hal - le - lu-ja! Of Je - sus sing and Ma - ri - a.

Index of first lines and titles

(Titles that differ from first lines appear in italics.)